FLASH FILSTRUP

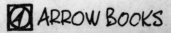

ARROW BOOKS

D1323160

FLASH FILSTRUP

The Fastest Overcoat in Town

by PETER PLANT

Arrow Books Limited
17–21 Conway Street, London W1P 6JD

An imprint of the Hutchinson Publishing Group

London Melbourne Sydney Auckland
Johannesburg and agencies
throughout the world

First published in Great Britain 1982

Made and printed in Great Britain
by The Anchor Press Ltd
Tiptree, Essex

ISBN 0 09 929080 4

FOREWORD BY MR. FILSTRUP

I'VE BEEN A PERVERT FOR OVER TWENTY YEARS. I'VE WORN OUT SIXTEEN
OVERCOATS AND FORTY-SEVEN PAIRS OF RUNNING SHOES. I'VE SEEN A LOT
OF UPS AND DOWNS AND, BELIEVE ME, IT AIN'T NO GAME FOR SOFTIES.
BUT IF IT'S TOUGH, THERE ARE STILL THE THINGS THAT MAKE IT WORTHWHILE.
LIKE THE CAMARADERIE AT THE PERVERTS' CLUB AND MINI-GOLF ON A
SATURDAY NIGHT. THE LOVE AND DEVOTION OF MY GIRLFRIEND BARBRA, THE
BEST CHICK A PERVERT COULD EVER WANT. THE LOYALTY OF MY BEST PAL BERNIE.
EVEN THO' HE'S STRAIGHT HE KNOWS I'VE NEVER HELD THAT AGAINST HIM.
WHEN THE GUY ASKED IF HE COULD PUT THIS BOOK TOGETHER ABOUT ME I
MADE ONE STIPULATION: 'I WANT NOTHING HIDDEN', I SAID. 'EVERYTHING HAS
GOTTA BE RIGHT OUT FRONT FOR PEOPLE TO SEE.'
I JUST WANT EVERYBODY TO KNOW THAT NO MATTER HOW YOU LOOK AT IT
I'M THE FASTEST OVERCOAT IN TOWN.
HASSA!

FLASH

YOU- YOU HORRIBLE FILTHY, DISGUSTING FOUL-MINDED DEGENERATED LITTLE PERVERT!

A COUPLE MORE LIKE THAT AND WE'LL CALL IT A NIGHT.

HA-SA!

DAMN! THIS LIGHT IS TERRIBLE! I BETTER GIVE IT A HALF-SECOND MORE EXPOSURE.

HASSA!

YAAGH!

IN THIS BUSINESS, IT'S THE FINE ADJUSTMENTS THAT MAKE ALL THE DIFFERENCE.

THERE AIN'T ROOM ENOUGH ON THIS STREET FOR THE TWO OF US, FILSTRUP. THIS IS A SHOWDOWN.

HAVEN'T YOU HEARD? I'M THE FASTEST OVERCOAT IN TOWN.

I HEARD YOU WAS GETTIN' **SLOW**, FILSTRUP.

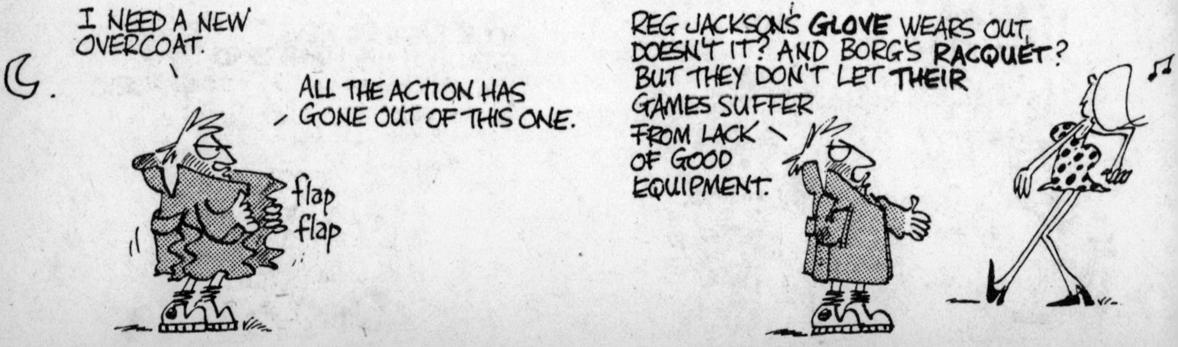
I NEED A NEW OVERCOAT.
ALL THE ACTION HAS GONE OUT OF THIS ONE.
flap
flap
REG JACKSON'S **GLOVE** WEARS OUT, DOESN'T IT? AND BORG'S **RACQUET**? BUT THEY DON'T LET **THEIR** GAMES SUFFER FROM LACK OF GOOD EQUIPMENT.

IMMIGRATION
PLEASE PRESENT YOUR DOCUMENTS

HASSA!

flip

STAMP
STAMP

IMMIGRATION
PLEASE PRESENT YOUR DOCUMENTS

ET... VOILA!

OKAY, OKAY, YOU'RE A YUGOSLAVIAN FLAGPOLE SITTER.

COULD YOU
PLEASE POINT
ME IN THE
DIRECTION OF
WIMPLE STREET?

HASSA!

THANK YOU.

PEOPLE LIKE HER GIVE ME
A PAIN IN THE ASS.

HASSA!

NO. BUT
WILL **I** DO?

flip

EEAGH!

I GUESS THAT'LL BE
HER LAST DING-DONG
OF THE DAY.

OKAY, FELLAS. WE'RE HERE TO DISCUSS THE LACKLUSTRE PERFORMANCE OF THE MEMBERS DURING THE PAST MONTH IN THE STREET.

BAM!

PERVERTS CLUB
MEMBERS ONLY

MAYBE WE AIN'T GETTIN' ENOUGH EXPOSURE! HA-HA-HA!

PERVERTS CLUB
MEMBERS ONLY

HOLY SNAPPERS, FLASH! WHAT HAPPENED?

EVER HEAR OF THE GRINWALD ATHLETIC CLUB LADIES' TRACK TEAM?

YEAH.

YESTERDAY AFTERNOON I SAW THEM ALL JOGGIN' UP FREMONT AVENUE.

shake
shake

WOULD YOU
CARE TO DONATE
A LITTLE SOME-
THING TO THE
CROXLEY
FOUNDATION?

HOW ABOUT THIS?

OHMYJESUS.

TELL CROXLEY
I DIDN'T HAVE
ANYTHING SMALLER.

HAAAA-

AWK!

-SA!

ZAZ

THERE GOES ONE PIGEON
WHO'LL THINK TWICE ABOUT
LEAVING THE FLOCK.

HEY! I MADE THE NEWSPAPERS!

"Woman Sees Pervert"

Mrs. Fanny Freswell reported that a man indecently exposed himself to her last night in the park. "Without a doubt," she said, "it was the most disgusting, deranged, and perverse display of obscenity I have ever seen!"

AND I THOUGHT I WAS HAVING AN **OFF-NIGHT!**

HAND ME MY
THREE IRON.

PSST.

HASSA.

WACK!

YOU'RE IN THE ROUGH ABOUT TWO HUNDRED YARDS FROM THE GREEN.

HASSA! flip

AAGH!
EEEG! OHNO! WOOF!
SCRAMBLE! IYEE!
WHACK! SCRATCH!
ARF! BUMP! OOH!
GRAPPLE! THUMP!
SQUISH!! RING! ≡
WHUMP! OWCH!

FOR A MINUTE THERE
I HAD A CAPTIVE
AUDIENCE.

HELLO? WHAT'S THIS?
A YOUNG LADY STANDING
ALL ALONE AT THE
BUS STOP?

I WONDER HOW
MY DISTANCE IS.

fling

CHORKLE.
CHORKLE.

I'VE NEVER SEEN ANYONE
SO GLAD TO SEE A BUS
COME ALONG.

HEY! I'VE ALMOST BEATEN HI-HO O'HOOLIHAN'S RECORD OF THIRTY-THREE IN TWELVE HOURS!!
I'VE GOT SIX MINUTES TO FLASH MYSELF INTO THE RECORD BOOK.
flash
flash
flash

ERG.

HASSA!

SHE CAME ALONG JUST IN
TIME. THAT EXPANSION
BRACELET
WAS
BEGINNING
TO PINCH.

AAGH!
OGH!
EEGH!

I FLASHED HER AND RAN AWAY WITHOUT GIVING HER DIRECTIONS.

YOU SHOULDN'T LET IT UPSET YOU.

BUT I WAS GOING THAT WAY, ANYHOW!

I **DID** STICK IT OUT
AT LAW SCHOOL, BARBRA.
ABOUT **TWICE A DAY**!

HEY, BARBRA! WHADDYA SAY WE GO FOR A STEAK AT DINO'S?
ONLY IF YOU PROMISE TO BEHAVE YOURSELF.
WHAT DO YOU MEAN BY THAT?
LAST TIME YOU REALLY EMBARRASSED ME WHEN YOU EXPOSED YOURSELF TO THE CHECKROOM GIRL!

I DIDN'T DO ANYTHING
OF THE KIND, BARBRA...

I WAS MERELY SHOWING HER WHY
I DIDN'T THINK IT WOULD BE A
VERY GOOD IDEA IF I CHECKED
MY OVERCOAT.

HEY, BARBRA. WILL YOU
DO ME A FAVOUR?

SURE, FLASH.

I WANNA TRY OUT
MY TERRIFYIN' NEW
SUPERFLASH ON YOU.

OKAY. GO AHEAD.

KYA-**HOY!**

flap

I LIKE THE IDEA OF THE SHARK'S TOOTH, BUT THE FALSE NOSE AND GLASSES IS A BIT OVER THE TOP.

HA-SA!

HA-SO!

...AND BY GETTING HYSTERICAL, THE WAY YOU DID, YOU'RE JUST GIVING THESE PERVERTS THE REACTION THEY WANT.

WAAA! HE'S LEFT ME!!

WAAAAAA! HE'S GONE! SOB!

OOOG!

JUMPIN' GOOLIES, FLASH! WHAT **HAPPENED**?

I WAS WALKIN' DOWN FINSBURY AVENUE. YOU KNOW THE STREET WITH ALL THE OFFICE BUILDINGS?

OOG!

YEAH.
YEAH.

FLASH FILSTRUP'S
SCHOOL OF THE FLASH

OPEN, CLOSE, THREE, FOUR!
OPEN, CLOSE, THREE, FOUR!
COME ON! LEAN INTO IT! ARCH
THAT BACK!!

FLASH FILSTRUP'S
SCHOOL OF THE FLASH

WHAT'S THE MATTER WITH
YOU, SPENCER? SHY?

I'M EMBARRASSED ABOUT THE TATTOO ON MY DINKY.

WHAT'S THE TATTOO?

A RELIEF MAP OF THE SOVIET UNION.

FLASH FILSTRUP'S
SCHOOL OF THE FLASH

OPEN, CLOSE, THREE, FOUR!
OPEN, CLOSE, THREE, FOUR!

WHAT DO YOU THINK YOU'RE
DOIN', MICKEY? TAKING A
HOLIDAY?

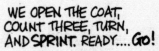

FLASH!!
WHUMP! WHAP! FWUMP!

IT MIGHT BE A GOOD IDEA
IF WE ALL SPRINT IN THE
SAME DIRECTION.

FLASH FILSTRUP'S
SCHOOL OF THE FLASH

OPEN, CLOSE, THREE, FOUR.
OPEN, CLOSE, THREE, FOUR.

RAISE THE RIGHT
KNEE AND—

NA-NA-NA
NOO-NOO
NEE-NEE
NHA-NHAY-G-G-G
WAH-WAH-WAH....

SHE WAS EITHER
VERY, VERY NERVOUS,
OR PRACTISING HER
GERMAN ON ME...

"PROVIDED IT IS NOT ABUSED, THE FLASH WILL BECOME
ONE OF MAN'S GREATEST ARTISTIC EXPRESSIONS"

Flash Filstrup.